EXTREME CAREERS

FIGHTER PILOTS

Life at Mach Speed

Allison Stark Draper

the rosen publishing group's
rosen
central

Published in 2001 by The Rosen Publishing Group, Inc.
29 East 21st Street, New York, NY 10010

Library of Congress Cataloging-in-Publication Data

Draper, Allison Stark.
Fighter pilots : life at mach speed / by Allison Stark Draper.— 1st ed.
p. cm. — (Extreme careers)
Includes bibliographical references and index.
ISBN 0-8239-3366-0
1. Fighter plane combat—United States—Juvenile literature. 2. Fighter pilots—Vocational guidance—United States—Juvenile literature. 3. United States—Armed Forces—Military life—Juvenile literature. [1. Fighter pilots—Vocational guidance. 2. United States. Armed Forces—Military life. 3. Vocational guidance.]
I. Title. II. Series.
UG703 .D73 2001
358.4'3'023—dc21
00-012711

Manufactured in the United States of America

Contents

Sky High

*Y*ou could hear them before you could see them—a high, thin whine shrilling over a deeper rumble and rising to a scream as they appeared over a ridge of spiky, black trees. There were four of them, flying in a tight diamond formation. They moved in concert, all four banking left and right in a series of seamless swoops as they crossed the field beyond the runway. They vanished over a hill and then circled back, dropping altitude and gaining roar. As they reached the center of the field, they dipped. You could make out their long, pointed snouts and sleek wings. The two side jets banked hard away

4

from the others, and the four airplanes rolled; the pilots' white helmets gleaming through the glass bubbles of their cockpits.

Then they started climbing. They rose so steeply they stood nearly on their tails. After a minute, they were almost out of sight—tiny silver triangles flashing high in the heavens. Then they descended, two dropping fast and spinning like tops, the other two tracing lazy aerobatic loops down through the sky. When they were no more than a thousand feet up, they formed a line at the far end of the field. One after another, they turned toward the runway and set down—their engines rattling the bones of everybody watching, their tires pummeling the tarmac in a hot screech of burnt rubber—and then hurtled back into the sky, the two red flame plumes of the afterburners scorching from the tailpipes. After the fourth airplane had come and gone, roaring back across the field and over the ridge, we stood there, dizzy with the heady smell of jet exhaust, hot metal, and burning oil, wondering what we would have to do to get to fly one of those things.

Fighter planes, like the F-15 Strike Eagle shown here, are the fastest, most sophisticated airplanes in the world.

The Lure of the Jet

Over the course of the twentieth century, flying changed from the crazy pursuit of futuristic dreamers to something only slightly more exciting than boarding a bus. For many people, a plane is no more than the quickest armchair between two geographical points. For others, however, the thrill of flying has grown immeasurably with advances in technology. An airplane was once a tricky collection of silk wings, taut wires, and a sort of aerial car engine. Now a sleek, muscular, superpowered jet is capable of breaking the sound barrier, flying at Mach speed, climbing tens of thousands of feet above the earth, and landing, with no visibility, in heaving seas, on the tiny target of an aircraft carrier. The fighter plane is the fastest, most sophisticated airplane on the planet. It is also among the most difficult to fly. Fighter pilots are highly trained members of the air force, the navy, and the marines. Although fighter planes are designed and built by private companies, like Boeing and Lockheed Martin, their single purpose is national defense. They, and their pilots, belong to the armed services.

If you want to become a fighter pilot, the simple desire to fly is not enough. You need to focus on your education as well as on your flight training. The average fighter pilot has a solid academic track record as well as a strong athletic record. You can start preparing for a career as a fighter pilot when you are still in high school by speaking with your guidance counselor about which courses will put you on the right track. Science and math are absolute requirements in the technologically advanced armed services; the more classes you take in these areas, the better prepared you will be. All of the American armed services encourage continuing education. If you are sure about your desire to pursue a military career, you should explore earning a degree while on active duty or attending college and entering a program like the Reserve Officers' Training Corps (ROTC). This program can also help you pay for college.

You may want to consider attending a school directly affiliated with the navy or the air force, like the United States Naval Academy or Air Force Academy. You can also enlist directly in one of the services after college, or before college with the intention of continuing your education while serving. To join the air force or the navy, you must be at least eighteen years old, or seventeen with a parent's or guardian's permission.

The History of Aviation Warfare

The first step in using aircraft as a weapon of war occurred on June 26, 1794. In the Battle of Fleurus, in which France fought Austria and the Netherlands, the French used a tethered hot-air balloon as a very high observation tower to monitor the battlefield and direct artillery fire. The balloonists were able to watch the movements of the enemy at a great distance and report down to their own side. Some military strategists saw real possibilities for the wartime uses of flying machines. Others thought the idea was ridiculous.

In the first major aerial attack, it seemed the skeptics may have been right. It was 1849 and the Austrians were attacking Venice, Italy. They planned to direct a force of armed, but unmanned, hot-air balloons over the center of the city. When the balloons reached the target point, they would release timed bombs. Unfortunately for the Austrians, the wind changed and the balloons blew harmlessly off track. It seemed that what the world needed was a more responsive aircraft. Within fifty years, the world had one. By the early twentieth century, engine-powered airplanes were a reality and were becoming sophisticated enough to have a real effect on the nature and strategy of war.

The Air Force

By the time World War I broke out, the United States Air Force had been born. The first job of the air force pilots, like the early balloonists at Fleurus, was reconnaissance. Airplanes provided an aerial view of enemy movements without endangering their pilots. This was a big improvement over crawling through the undergrowth behind enemy lines to spy. Of course, the use of reconnaissance planes was not restricted to one side or another. It soon became clear that stopping the enemy from figuring out what you were doing was at least as crucial as figuring out what they were doing.

There was no question that the best way to stop the enemy was to shoot them down in the air. As a result, airplanes began to carry machine guns.

This was a great idea, but it created problems for airplane designers. Not only did they have to create a machine that could fly, but one that could carry the weight of a pilot, a gunner, and a heavy machine gun. In addition, it had to be able to turn quickly enough in the air to target and shoot an enemy while moving fast enough to stay clear of enemy fire. One thing that became startlingly obvious was that techno-logy only went so far. The real fly-or-die success of a fighter

The United States Air Force first used airplanes to spy on enemy movements during World War I.

plane depended upon the skill, quick thinking, and coolheadedness of its pilot.

Birth of the Fighter Pilot

Fighter pilots were fast becoming the hotshots of the war. Soon there was a ranking system, invented by the French, who designed and flew some of the best airplanes of the era. The title of "fighter ace" was

The exploits of World War I fighter pilots provided much inspiration for Hollywood's war movies.

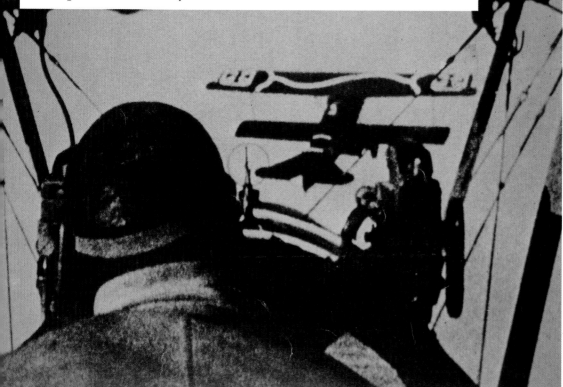

bestowed on pilots who shot down five or more enemy planes. Fighter pilots started to gain a kind of international glamour all their own. The system remained intact through World War II, when improvements in planes and weapons led to massive escalation in individual scores. Scorekeeping was complicated and varied from country to country, but it seems likely that the world's all-time highest-scoring fighter ace was a German named Erich Hartmann. Hartmann shot down 352 planes in World War II.

After World War II ended, there was a lot of money in America for military training. The nation entered a period of great faith in the might and right of the American military. This meant that it was important to train—and fund—as many likely young soldiers and pilots as possible. Anyone with a couple of years of college, 20/20 vision, and a basic aptitude to fly an airplane could join the air force or enter the naval aviation cadet program and become a navy pilot. By the early 1990s, however, this began to change somewhat. The military grew smaller. There were fewer and fewer slots in the air force and navy flight-training programs. The competition grew fierce. Soon, only college graduates—preferably those from

Breaking Barriers

There have always been important and groundbreaking women pilots—women like Amelia Earhart and Beryl Markham in the early days of aviation—but for many years, there were none in the military. The first woman to insist on the need for a women's air force service was Jackie Cochran. When she did this, during World War II, Cochran already had an impressive aviation track record. In 1934, she became the first female test pilot, flying and testing the first turbo-charger ever installed on a civilian aircraft engine. In addition, she helped design the first oxygen mask and was the first person to fly above 20,000 feet wearing one. She also set three speed records and, in 1938, set a world altitude record of 33,000 feet.

As World War II loomed, Cochran saw a need for women pilots in the military. She talked First Lady Eleanor Roosevelt into helping establish the Women Airforce Service Pilots (WASPs). She recruited more than 1,000 women to the force and supervised their training and service until they were disbanded in 1944. She herself became the first female transatlantic bomber pilot.

In the wake of World War II, as now, access to state-of-the-art fighter planes was exclusively military, but Cochran was a friend of General Chuck Yeager. She flew in an F-86 Sabre jet at Edwards Air Force Base and became the first woman to break the sound barrier. Yeager (the first person to break the sound barrier) went along for the ride. Cochran also set a world speed record of 1,429 mph in 1964, when she was well over fifty years of age.

a military academy or a program like ROTC—were making it into training programs.

Superstars

The people accepted into flight-training programs were superstars. They were smart, athletic, and highly educated. They did not do drugs or tangle with the law. Some of them were bona fide rocket scientists. Older air force and navy officers and pilots were sometimes skeptical. What did good grades have to do with flying a jet? Would these brainy college grad-uates really make better fighter pilots? The answer is complicated. Some people have the ability to fly an airplane the way others can play basketball or sing on key easily. They do not necessarily need to have straight As in their aeronautical (airplane) engineering classes to be good fighter pilots. On the other hand, the technology of the military fighter jet has become a lot more complicated and requires a great deal of technical and scientific knowledge.

The state-of-the-art fighter plane is twenty times faster than that of a World War II ace. It is able to fly six times as high and has radar- and communication-enhanced visibility that has transformed the airplane into a whole new machine. Modern fighter planes are larger. They have sophisticated weapons and complicated safety features. The modern fighter pilot needs to understand far more about navigation and weaponry than the twentieth century's aces. In addition, as the machinery has become increasingly expensive, the willingness of the world's air forces to let just anyone climb into a cockpit has decreased radically. When they let you loose in one of their multimillion-dollar jets, they want you to have a real idea of how the plane works.

The job of fighter pilot—and today this seems unbelievable—was once a refuge for those who did not quite make it into such established branches of the military as the light cavalry. Today, fighter pilots are an elite group, standing at the pinnacle of the world's armed forces.

2

Becoming a Fighter Pilot

How does a person decide to become a fighter pilot? What is the long road from climbing into the cockpit of an air force jet on a school field trip at age ten to actually growing up and flying a jet of your own? For some pilots, flying jets is a dream that starts in childhood after hearing sonic booms crack overhead or watching maneuvers at a military base. For others, the idea develops much later. They rise through the ranks of the military academies, attending the U. S. Air Force Academy or Naval Academy with the intention of joining the armed services and, once they're in, realize that flight training is what they want.

Others attend nonmilitary private or state schools. They participate in ROTC with the intention of doing a small amount of military time and then returning to civilian life. To their surprise, the challenge, camaraderie, and work with the cutting-edge technology of the military proves so appealing that they stay, earning commissions and rising through the military ranks.

More than one civilian has fallen in love with flying in a single-engine propeller plane on a local airfield. Their pursuit of that sense of freedom and power has led them to the ultimate endpoint: the fighter jet. And the way to fly the best planes in the world is to join the military.

Serious Business

A military career can be rewarding and exhilarating, but it is also a tough and serious commitment. Flying for the services is not the pursuit of hotshots. Modern fighter pilots work hard and follow the rules. They graduate in the top 10 percent of their high school and college classes. When they become commissioned officers, they remain in the top 10 percent, holding out for high honors, such as an

Over time, the United States Air Force backed away from its opposition to women becoming fighter pilots. As a result, a growing number of female students find their names on fighter-jet rosters.

assignment to flight training and then to fighter training. Assignments are based on merit. Students who finish at the top of their classes choose flight assignments first. Almost inevitably, they choose to fly fighter jets. This means that for those who do not make the cut, there are alternate assignments flying transport airplanes and helicopters. The current bias is toward students who excel at science and engineering, but there is some room on the tiny fighter-jet roster for students with other strengths. Although the higher-ups are sometimes surprised, it is not always the rocket scientists who make the best fighter pilots.

The Basics

The basic process of flying a plane—not a fighter jet like an FA-18 Hornet, but, say, a single-engine propeller plane—is surprisingly straightforward. Almost anyone who can drive a car can fly an airplane. A plane stays aloft because the engine creates thrust and pulls the plane forward. When the plane is moving, air flows over its wings. This creates lift. Lift offsets the plane's weight, which is defined as a force due to gravity, which pulls the plane toward the earth. Airplanes are designed to glide. If the engine in a small airplane fails, the plane may be able to glide to a bumpy but nonfatal "dead stick" landing (in the old days, pilots steered with sticks instead of wheels) because the engineless descent of the plane continues to create airflow around the plane's wings.

In order to take off, the pilot pushes the engine to full power and lets the airplane race down the runway. When it has accumulated enough speed, the pilot pulls back on the stick. This lifts the nose of the plane into the air. It is important not to rise too steeply because the air will not be able to create enough lift around the airplane's wings and the plane will stall. This means it will stop moving forward and drop back to the ground. Instead, just after lifting off the ground, the pilot pushes the nose forward just a touch and continues upward at a shallower angle, steadily gaining speed. As the plane moves faster, it can rise more steeply.

When the airplane reaches the desired altitude, the pilot levels out. To steer, the pilot turns both the wheel and the tail rudder, which is controlled by foot pedals. To descend, the pilot lowers the nose and uses the flaps on the wings to slow or control the speed of the descent. To land, the pilot descends to just above the runway and then pulls the nose back up, flying level along the runway but slowing the engine and gradually letting the plane drop. First, the back wheels touch gently down, then the front wheels. Now the plane is driving along the runway, or "taxiing," once again returned to the ground.

3
Flight Training

The first thing you will learn, when you make the cut into the fighter training program, is that before you can fly a particular fighter plane, you need to explore and memorize every detail of its capabilities and systems. Every plane makes its own special demands on a pilot. Regardless of background, flight hours clocked, or skill, there is no substitute for total familiarity with a piece of machinery. Certainly your average fighter pilot can fly more than one kind of airplane, but the difference between flying an F-14 Tomcat and flying an FA-18 Hornet is far greater than the difference between driving a Ford pickup and driving a Jeep.

When flight students qualify for fighter-jet training, they qualify for an entire course of training in one particular airplane. They live and breathe that airplane until they qualify for missions in it or fail out of the course. Every inch of a plane needs to be burned into the waking and sleeping minds of its pilots. They need to know the location and utility of every control and instrument, its speeds under differ-ent stresses, its maneuverability in different attitudes (positions of the plane), and the complex compo-nents of its "personality." And those are just the details you can see. Students also need to commit to

USAF flight training is not limited to flying a particular airplane. The fighter pilot also learns about aviation maintenance, the military justice system, radio protocol, and a wide range of social issues.

memory the map of their airplane's electrical system schematics and the diagrams of its fuel and hydraulic systems.

One on One

The true fighter plane has only one pilot who flies, navigates, and, in combat, attacks. Therefore, the pilot needs to understand every aspect of the plane's flight. The pilot needs both to fly and to navigate, using the plane's six DDIs, or digital display indicators, to navigate not only the routes,

A flight instructor sits beside his student as she operates a flight simulator at the U.S. Naval Air Station in Pensacola, Florida.

but also the potential route changes of the airplane, as well as the routes of its weapons.

This is a lot to handle. It necessitates keeping an immense amount of information organized in one's head. In addition, some modern fighters use a design system called HOTAS, or "hands on throttle and stick." This means that nearly all of the plane's flight and fire commands are located on the throttle (in the left hand) and the stick (in the right). There are countless combinations of button and switch commands that enable the pilot to do everything, from steering to talking on the radio to shooting at an enemy. This can be dangerous because in a tense situation a pilot might panic and lose control of the throttle and stick system, accidentally activating the autopilot instead of the radio or firing guns instead of dropping a bomb.

Much of this instruction is computerized. In computer-assisted instruction, or CAI, students sit in little booths with computers that test their knowledge of the plane to which they have been assigned. The computers respond to their individual skill levels, forcing them to work harder in weak areas and advancing them quickly through strong ones. There are also lectures in which flight instructors discuss

Flight simulators test a student's ability to use all of a plane's instruments and flight data displays without risking loss of life or machine.

important, non-plane-specific topics such as aviation maintenance procedures, the military justice system, radio protocol, and community issues such as race relations and AIDS prevention.

The Glass Cockpit

After two weeks of computer drilling in the ins and outs of the engine systems, instruments, and aerodynamics of their airplane, each member of a fighter training class climbs into a version of an actual cockpit. This is a simulator called an operational flight trainer, or OFT. It enables students to "fly" a fighter plane before actually lifting the nation's multimillion-dollar investments off the ground.

The simulator lessons are mentally demanding and, sometimes, unnervingly real. Students emerge drained and sweaty from long sessions in which they use all of the instruments and flight data displays they have struggled to memorize, all while looking into a clear bubble at a view of the airport, horizon, and sky they see every day. It is grueling but also thrilling—a major step on the way to the real thing.

Fighter Pilots: Life at Mach Speed

Finally, climbing into the cockpit of a real fighter jet is almost unreal. Modern fighters are equipped with what is called a glass cockpit. This means the flight instruments that show flight data like attitude and altitude (height above sea level) are all computerized. The interior looks kind of like a high-tech computer game. Actually, it looks exactly like the simulator.

4

Ready for Takeoff

Training planes for single-seat fighter jets are almost always two-seaters. They are tandem planes, which means one seat is located behind the other. For first flights, an instructor rides in the backseat. The instructor will provide advice and criticism, or step in to keep the student out of trouble, but for the most part, the work of the flight is up to the student.

The student prepares for the flight by recording all the flight data. This includes flight times, radio frequencies for communications, the number and identification of the plane and identities of the pilot and instructor/passenger, weather conditions, the area of the flight, alternate routes and landing destinations in case of unforeseen problems, and the amount of fuel

Torso harness

Helmet with radio

Flight boots

G suit

required. Once the flight data is prepared and approved, the student can gear up for the flight. Flight clothes include heavy flight boots and a G suit. A "G" is a unit of force of the earth's gravity. Walking around at sea level, a person feels the force of one G. Under the pressure of very fast acceleration, as on a roller coaster or in a fighter plane, G-force increases.

When a jet flies up steeply or pulls out of a dive, the pressure on a pilot can rise to four or five Gs. This causes the blood to drain out of the pilot's head leading to a woozy gray-out, or the full blackout of unconsciousness. A G suit responds to an increase in G-force by filling with air around a pilot's legs and abdomen. This squeezes the blood back up toward the brain. The pilot also wears a torso harness with fittings that attach to seat straps in the cockpit, and an SV-2 survival vest containing an inflatable life vest and ten pounds of important emergency equipment, such as flares, lights, a radio, a mirror, and water.

Once they are suited up, the instructor walks the student through the entire flight, from starting the engine to landing on the runway. No step is too tiny to be important, and the flight review includes details such as entering the cockpit properly and adjusting

The flight instructor sits behind a student in the tandem plane to provide advice and criticism, or to take over if the student has trouble.

the seat. The instructor and the student also discuss emergency procedures such as ejection, spin recovery, and tactics for responding to engine failure.

Preflight

Before flying an airplane, a pilot must inspect it in a procedure called a preflight check. A fighter plane preflight includes checking landing gear struts, tires, panel fasteners, and weapons pylons. As on all airplanes, it is important to check fuel mixture and level, engine inlets and exhausts, and any leaks, cracks, or dents. Jet engines are easily damaged by foreign objects, such as nuts and screws that their intakes can vacuum off the hangar floor.

When the preflight is complete, the pilot straps in and arms the ejection seat. Strapping in means securing shoulder and waist straps to the torso harness and fastening retention straps. Retention straps are

A flight instructor watches his student as she performs a preflight check.

"Alpha, Bravo, Charlie"

When pilots speak with air traffic controllers, they announce their planes' call numbers, which like license plate numbers include both numerals and letters. To reduce the possibility of listeners mishearing letters, both military and civilian pilots use a phonetic alphabet.

A—Alpha
B—Bravo
C—Charlie
D—Delta
E—Echo
F—Foxtrot
G—Golf
H—Hotel
I—India
J—Juliet
K—Kilo
L—Lima
M—Mike

N—November
O—Oscar
P—Papa
Q—Quebec
R—Romeo
S—Sierra
T—Tango
U—Uniform
V—Victor
W—Whiskey
X—X ray
Y—Yankee
Z—Zulu

The number nine is pronounced "niner" to avoid confusion with *nein*, the German word for "no." Zero is always pronounced "zero" and never "oh."

designed to keep the legs still during ejection. Next, an oxygen hose and radio connection are joined to the torso harness. Then the G suit plugs in so that it can fill with air in the event of an increase in Gs. Once successfully strapped in and prepared, the student activates the various flaps, brakes, and controls so that a ground crew member can make sure they are fully operational.

The student radios to air traffic control for permission, taxis to the head of the runway, and waits for confirmation for takeoff. When takeoff permission is confirmed, the student pushes both throttles all the way forward—possibly, depending on the plane, all the way into afterburner. (An afterburner creates extra thrust—on the order of 40 percent more—by widening the exhaust nozzles of the jet engines and injecting raw fuel into the exhaust blasts.) When the afterburner kicks in, the airplane roars as two plumes of flame explode from its exhaust nozzles and then tears down the runway like a race car. Now the student "rotates," pulling back on the stick and shooting the plane into the air. In the thrill of lifting off, the instructor may have to remind the student to draw in the landing gear, which suffers serious damage at high airspeeds.

A fighter pilot must know how to perform various dogfight maneuvers, including barrel rolls, aileron rolls, and the split-S.

Aloft in a Fighter

Once aloft, the student is ready to put the fighter jet through its paces. All of the instruments and electrical systems can be memorized on land, but there is no simulator substitute for the adrenaline of real-sky aerobatics. These include the long, smooth corkscrews of barrel rolls; the dizzy aileron rolls, which twist the airplane like a top; and big, vertical somersaulting loops. Apart from the navy's Blue Angels, who perform these maneuvers in a virtuoso display that highlights their beauty, most pilots hone these moves for success in the dogfight. In the split-S, the plane rolls upside down and plunges into a nosedive that pulls out at the bottom of a loop. This is a handy way to change direction quickly under fire. The modern fighter jet is also capable of slow flight. This means it can almost hang in the air vertically, standing on its tail, at the comparatively slow speed of 100 knots, or 100 nautical miles per hour.

The most difficult part of flying a fighter jet is landing it. This is true with most planes. Skill in this area is particularly important for navy fighter pilots because they need to be able to bring an airplane down on the tiny, rocking, sea-slick surface of an aircraft carrier, day or night, regardless of visibility.

When a pilot lands correctly, the plane's four-foot tailhook snags one of four wires stretched across the deck and stops the plane. The aid to this seemingly impossible task is a Fresnel lens. The lens is a rectangle in which an amber ball is outlined in green lights. The ball shows the position of the plane in relation to the runway. To land the plane, the pilot must follow the

For student pilots, landing a plane with the aid of a
Fresnel lens is perhaps the trickiest element in flying.

ball. If the ball is too high, the plane is too high and
will fly off the far end of the aircraft carrier. If the ball is
too low, the plane is too low and will smack into the
aircraft carrier's near side and drop into the sea.
Keeping the ball centered is tricky.

Students and new pilots tend to overcompensate,
forcing the ball to swing violently from too high to
too low back to too high. The trick is to handle the
controls delicately, making minute adjustments and
responding to any slight shift on the ball's part with a

very slight opposite shift. To practice "flying the ball," pilots fly "touch-and-gos." This means landing on the runway and taking off again immediately, over and over again, in a long series of practice landings.

In addition, students need to practice emergency landings, like the engine-out approach in which they land with only one of two engines operating. Some students actually find landing with one engine easier because it allows them to do so using less power. The complex part is keeping the wings even.

One lands an airplane by pulling back on the stick. This raises the nose of the plane and tilts the stabilators on the tail. The stabilators create big, flat planes of drag against the air and work as brakes, helping to slow the plane so it can drop onto the runway. One frequent mistake novices make is to bring the stick back too far. This is particularly dangerous in certain fighters where the ejection loop is located at the far end of the stick. In one horrendous and frightening episode, a student pulled the stick back too far and got it caught in the ejection seat handle. When he pushed the stick forward again, he ejected right onto the runway.

5

Flying Solo

The first flight in a fighter jet is only an exhilarating introduction. Next comes a solo flight (with the instructor trailing in a chase plane), and then a radar navigation training mission from the backseat of a tandem-seat fighter. Radar navigation, or flying by instruments, enables a pilot to navigate at night or in heavy weather, when there is no physical visibility. All pilots are certified for visual flight rules (VFR); only pilots qualified for instrument flight rules (IFR) can fly at night or in clouds or fog.

After soloing and IFR qualification comes the backbreaking tactical phase of training. In the tactical phase, a student learns the mechanics of air-to-air refueling and complex combat maneuvers, practicing every new skill first in the simulator and then in the air. Combat maneuvers are the applied version of the aerobatic loops and rolls a first-timer does just to feel the power of the plane.

Formation Flying

The first stage of combat flying is formation flying. Any flight that involves more than one fighter is done in formation. The most excellent formation jets are capable of flying in formation only three feet apart. Now a student learns how these moves can keep a fighter jet above and behind another plane, in position for a kill. Finally, student fighter pilots have to learn the nature, use, and control systems of all the guns and bombs that their fighters carry.

In the early 1990s, the navy came up with a new tactical fighting idea: strike fighting. The strike fighter is a plane that can perform both air-to-air (plane against plane) and air-to-ground ("strike") missions. This means that fighter pilots learn not only the aerial combat tactics involved in a plane-on-plane dogfight, but also the strike tactics of attack planes. During the

Formation flying is the first stage of combat flying. It is also a fan favorite at military exhibitions.

strike phase of training, students learn to penetrate hostile territory by flying at a speed of 400 knots, 100 feet above the ground. They shoot guns, fire rockets, and drop real bombs on real targets, such as tanks, trucks, and buildings.

Bombing

A strike-training facility is a huge flat area, twenty miles square, with targets painted on the ground in

Saburo Sakai

During World War II, a Japanese fighter ace named Saburo Sakai became a living legend. Saburo Sakai was unusually gifted. He was also extremely well trained.

Prior to World War II, all Japanese naval pilots were trained at the Navy Fliers School at Tsuchiura, fifty miles northeast of Tokyo. They worked to improve their physical strength, stamina, coordination, and balance. Diving lessons prepared pilots for the way a fighter plane spins and rolls as it hurtles through the air. Once you were proficient at diving into water, you had to dive from a high tower to the ground, somersault two or three times, and land on your feet. Not every student survived this phase of training. One requirement for acceptance to Tsuchiura was extraordinary eyesight. As a pilot, it was necessary to spot enemy planes at a distance. To perfect this, students would pick out one of the brighter stars during daylight, whip their heads ninety degrees away and back, and find the star again instantly. Sakai said that in 200 air engagements, he was never surprised by an enemy attack.

In the open cockpit of a fighter plane, good peripheral vision was also crucial. To expand their range of vision, Sakai and his fellow students released flies beside their heads and reached up to grab them in their fists as they stared straight ahead. Sakai said that after several months of this, no fly was safe.

Sakai flew 200 combat missions and shot down sixty-four planes. He never lost a wingman, never overshot a landing, and never crash-landed. On one occasion he landed successfully despite paralyzing wounds in his left arm and leg, permanent blindness in his right eye, temporary loss of vision in his left eye, jagged pieces of metal in his back and chest, and the fragments of two 50-caliber machine-gun bullets embedded in his skull.

the shape of giant bull's-eyes. Students learn to dive in, drop practice bombs on the target, and zoom away. In the old days, dive-bombing was a matter of aiming the airplane at a target and struggling to maintain the same airspeed, dive angle, and wind correction. At a certain altitude, the pilot dropped the bombs and hoped for the best. Modern strike fighters are equipped with auto-bombing. The mission computer of the jet reads the current dive angle, velocity, and drift, calculates an ideal trajectory for the bomb, and launches the bomb

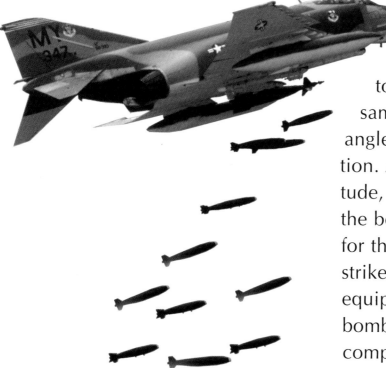

In strike training, students learn to dive in, drop practice bombs on the targets, and zoom away.

along the trajectory. The pilot has a display inside the cockpit that shows the bomb (a point of light) over a bull's-eye (the target).

The pilot levels the wings of the plane and aligns the light with the target. The computer decides when to release the bomb. This sounds easier than it is. If the pilot does not hold a smooth trajectory, the bomb's flight path will be skewed. Practice bombing involves approaching the targets from high and low angles and from every altitude. Students start with "dumb" bombs; once the bomb is launched, its trajectory is up to wind and fate. New "smart" weapons are guided after they are dropped. After they are launched, they can be directed to turn corners and enter doors and windows.

LAT

After bombing comes low-altitude training, or LAT. LAT is the most dangerous part of tactical aviation. LAT training begins at 500 feet. At this height, buildings and power lines are still visible before the airplane speeds past them. Eventually, the pilot gets

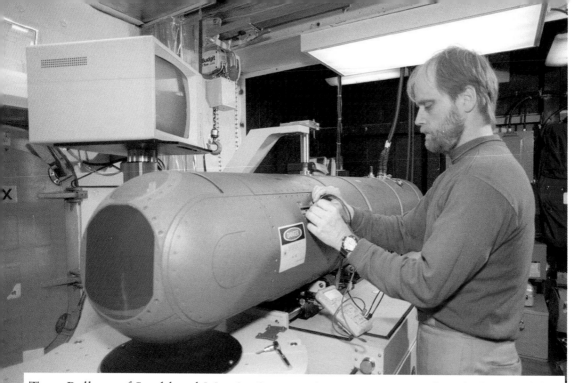

Tony Ballou, of Lockheed Martin Corporation, tests a smart bomb designed for use on the F-14 Tomcat during a Persian Gulf deployment on July 3, 1997.

the plane down to 100 feet. At this height and at a speed of 420 knots, the ground is a meaningless blur. Any error is probably final. A two-degree lowering of the plane's nose will plunge a pilot into a flaming wreck. One of the instruments that guards against this is an inertial reference platform, which knows exactly where the plane is in space at any time. It displays a constantly updated map on which the pilot can see both the plotted course and the actual path of the plane. Other LAT hazards include birds. Big birds, like buzzards and eagles, when hit at 400 knots, can bring a plane down as hard as a missile.

Strafing

After bombing and LAT comes strafing. Strafing means shooting with guns. It combines the target practice of bombing with the low-altitude maneuverability of LAT. A fighter pilot who is strafing has to get close to the ground on enemy turf and shoot to kill without being killed or losing track of the ground rising up beneath the plane. A practice strafing

Can Women Kill?

Historically, there has been resistance to women pilots in the armed services. When women were first cleared to fly combat missions, many male officers doubted whether women could or would kill. (One navy commander asked a female lieutenant in line for strike-fighter training whether she really believed she could kill another human being. She asked him if he had a gun.)

In 1996, research conducted by an air force team studied the effects of job stress on male and female pilots. The psychologists were surprised by the results. "We expected to find significant male/female differences . . . but we didn't," said Major Raymond E. King, Ph.D., of Armstrong Laboratory's Clinical Sciences Division, who conducted the study with Major Suzanne McGlohn, Ph.D. There appeared to be little psychological difference between men and women. "Men are generally thought to have stronger mechanical skills, while women are thought to possess stronger verbal skills, but we didn't find any evidence of that among air force pilots," said King. "The bottom line is, a pilot's a pilot."

Strafing combines flying at low altitude and shooting.

target might be a nylon banner, ten feet high and twenty feet wide. The pilot has to hit the banner from an altitude of 1,000 feet and at a downward angle of approach of fifteen degrees. A modern fighter enables a pilot to line up the target, but the pilot still needs a steady hand on the stick. While pressing close to the target makes it easier to get hits, it also makes it harder to pull out and rise back off the ground. Even worse, if a pilot comes in too low, the bullets can ricochet off the ground and smack back into the belly of the airplane.

Real Fighter Combat Training

Once a student has mastered formation flying, bombing, LAT, and strafing, it is time for air-to-air combat: real fighter combat training. At a navy air base in southern Florida, students in FA-18 Hornets are pitted against instructors masquerading as the enemy in FA-18s, F-5Es, and F-16s, all painted with sky camouflage paint (blues mottled like the greens of jungle combat gear or the browns of desert equipment). The adversary pilots use the tactics of such enemy fighter planes as MiG-21s, MiG-23s, or MiG-29s. They fly their American airplanes to mimic the performances of the enemy planes.

The first lesson is basic fighter maneuvering, or BFM. The simplest confrontation is a one-vee-one in which one plane goes up against another in plane-to-plane combat. In a typical confrontation, the airplanes first zoom past each other at the same altitude, several hundred feet apart. Each pilot wants to get behind the other to set up a clear shot without getting hit. The planes carry guns for close combat—less than one mile from the enemy—as well as missiles capable of downing a target at a distance of one to four miles.

When two planes face off, initially each tries to stay in front of the other. Sometimes, they start turning toward each other's tails, each trying to turn hard enough to get inside the other plane's turn and take a shot at its tail. They might also pass each other and twist around to pass each other again. As they approach, they pull their noses up until they are flying vertically. Eventually, if neither gives, one plane will slip into a spin, falling out of the sky like a huge hunk of metal. At a high enough altitude, it is usually possible to recover from such a fall in a modern fighter.

Good fighter pilots are able to keep track of their
position while tracking the movements of other planes.

One of the toughest parts of air-to-air combat is that it is difficult to anticipate. Every situation is different. Each demands sustained, split-second decision making. This differs from the complex planning and straightforward execution involved in air-to-ground or strike missions.

An air-to-air fight is also three-dimensional. The skill that allows fighter pilots to stay oriented in three dimensions at Mach speed is called situational awareness, or SA. Pilots with good SA are able to keep track of where they are in the sky while tracking the movements of other planes, both friendly and hostile. This skill is almost impossible to measure before a student fighter pilot is aloft in a dogfight. It is this special gift that propels a good pilot into the realm of the fighter ace.

A Major Commitment

If you do choose to follow the path of the fighter pilot, you need to be aware that the commitment is significant. If you start fighter training in your mid-twenties, right out of college, you will probably owe the government eight more years of service. This is because training fighter pilots is so expensive. If the navy or the air force puts you through college, teaches you to fly, and coaches you through strike fighter training, your education will cost about $2 million. School, training, and service will last approximately ten years.

At this point, many pilots decide whether or not to continue in the military. Continuing means more jets and higher rank. Getting out means finding a job as a commercial airline pilot or, if you are qualified, possibly as an aerospace engineer, making more money and keeping a routine schedule, which enables your family to worry a little less about your personal safety. It also means the end of your access to state-of-the-art military combat airplanes, and the loss of one of the coolest job descriptions in the world: fighter pilot.

Glossary

aerobatics Gymnastic feats of planes.

aerodynamics Science of the motion of air and objects in air.

aeronautics Art or science of flight.

aileron Movable portion of an airplane wing located at the trailing edge near the wingtip and used to control lateral movement.

altitude Height of a plane in the air.

attitude Tilt of a plane in the air.

bank The way a plane tilts when making a turn.

cockpit Where the seat and instruments are in a plane.

dogfight Fight in the air between two or more planes.

jet Plane powered by an engine that uses the surrounding air to burn fuel or by a rocket-type engine that carries both fuel and the oxygen needed for burning.

lift   Upward force on an airplane that opposes the pull of gravity.

Mach   Ratio between the speed of a plane and the speed of sound; a plane moving at the speed of sound is moving at Mach 1.

navigation   Science of directing planes from one place to another.

pitch   When the nose of a plane rises or falls in relation to the tail.

radar   Way of locating an object by emitting radio signals.

roll   To tip the wings from one side to the other while flying in a straight line.

rudder   Hinged flap on the tail of a plane that controls direction.

taxi   To move along the ground in a plane before takeoff or after landing.

thrust   Strong forward motion created by the backward discharge from a jet engine.

For More Information

The Joint Strike Fighter Program
http://www.jast.mil

Photos of Fighter Planes
http://www.allstar.fiu.edu/aero/meeteagl.htm
http://www.jast.mil/gallery/Gal_x32_1.thm
http://www.jastmil/gallery/gal_x35_1.htm

Principles of Flight
http://www.allstar.fiu.edu/aero/fltmidfly.htm

Super Hornet Information
http://www.boeing.com/defensespace/
    military/fa18ef/fa18ef.htm

United States Air Force
(800) 423-USAF (8723)
Web site: http://www.af.mil

United States Air Force Academy
HQ USAFA
Colorado Springs, CO 80840
(719) 333-3070
Web site: http://www.usafa.af.mil

United States Naval Academy
121 Blake Road
Annapolis, MD 21402-5000
Web site: http://www.usna.edu

United States Navy Blue Angels
Navy Flight Demonstration Squadron
390 San Carlos Road, Suite A
Pensacola, FL 32508-5508
(850) 452-BLUE (2583)
Web site: http://www.blueangels.navy.mil

In Canada

Air Force Association of Canada
P.O. Box 2460, Station "D"
Ottawa, ON K1P 5W6
(613) 992-7482
Web site: http://www.airforce.ca

Canadian Air Force/La Force Aérienne Canadienne
8 Wing Trenton
P.O. Box 1000 Station Forces
Astra, ON K0K 3W0
(808) 856-8488
Web site: http://www.airforce.dnd.ca

Canadian Forces Snowbirds (aerobatic team)
431 (AD) Sqn—Snowbirds
15 Wing
P.O. Box 5000
Moose Jaw, SK S6H 7Z8
Web site: http://www.snowbirds.dnd.ca

For Further Reading

Gandt, Robert. *Bogeys and Bandits: The Making of a Fighter Pilot.* New York: Viking Penguin, 1997.

Isby, David C. *Jane's How to Fly and Fight in the F/A-18 Hornet.* New York: HarperCollins, 1997.

Kennedy, Robert C. *Life as an Air Force Fighter Pilot.* New York: Children's Press, 2000.

Lopez, Donald S. *Fighter Pilot's Heaven: Flight Testing the Early Jets.* Washington: Smithsonian Institution Press, 1995.

Moore, John. *The Wrong Stuff: Flying on the Edge of Disaster.* Houston: Specialty Press, 1997.

Rosenkranz, Keith. *Vipers in the Storm: Diary of a Gulf War Fighter Pilot.* New York: McGraw-Hill, 1999.

Sakai, Saburo, Martin Caidin, and Fred Saito. *Samurai!* New York: Ibooks, 2001.

Smallwood, William. *Strike Eagle: Flying the F-15E in the Gulf War.* Washington: Brasseys, Inc., 1997.

Spears, Sally. *Call Sign Revlon: The Life and Death of Navy Fighter Pilot Kara Hultgreen.* Annapolis, MD: Naval Institute Press, 1998.

Spick, Mike. *The Complete Fighter Ace: All the World's Fighter Aces 1914–2000.* Mechanicsburg, PA: Stackpole Books, 1999.

Stout, Jay A. *Hornets over Kuwait.* Annapolis, MD: Naval Institute Press, 1997.

Wilcox, Robert K. *Wings of Fury: From Vietnam to the Gulf War—The Astonishing True Stories of America's Elite Fighter Pilots.* New York: Pocket Books, 1996.

Wolfe, Tom. *The Right Stuff.* New York: Farrar, Straus, Giroux, 1983.

Index

About the Author

Allison Stark Draper soloed on her sixteenth birthday in a Cessna 15. She lives in New York.

Photo Credits

Cover © Photori; p. 6 © Aero Graphics, Inc./Corbis; pp. 11, 12, 19, 23, 30, 32, 33, 36, 38, 42, 44, 48–49, 51 © Photori; p. 14 © Deutsche Presse/Archive Photos; pp. 24, 26 © Yogi, Inc./Corbis; p. 46 © AP Photo World Wide/Navy News.

Design and Layout

Les Kanturek